WACKY COMPARISONS

HOW TALL?

by Mark Weakland illustrated by Igor Sinkovec

T0100805

How tall is a PENGUIN?

How tall is a SKUNK?

Is either as tall as a TREE or CHIPMUNK?

A GIRAFFE, a DINO, a SOCCER BALL—

Time to discover how short and how tall!

PICTURE WINDOW BOOKS
a capstone imprint

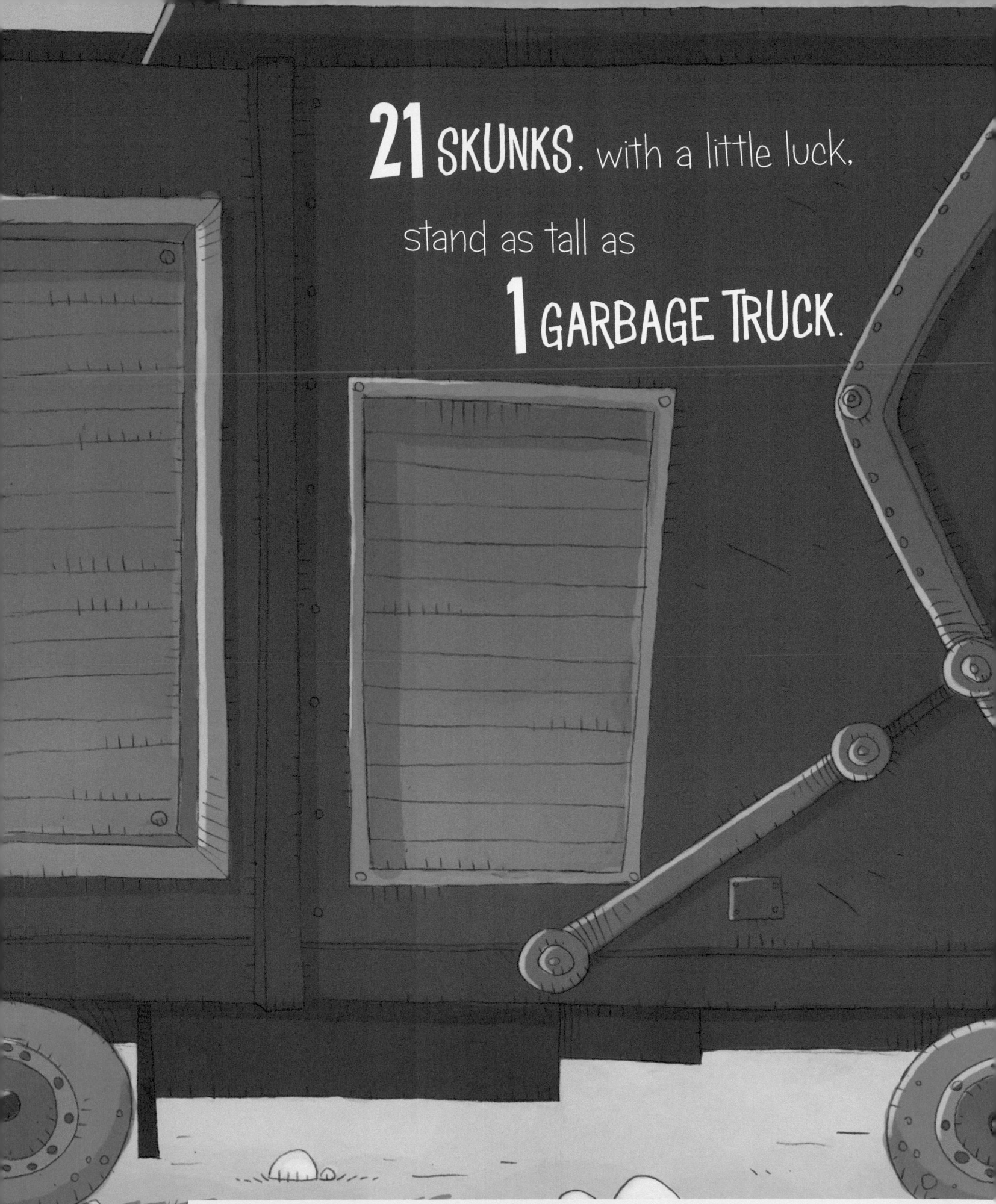

21 SKUNKS, with a little luck,
stand as tall as
1 GARBAGE TRUCK.

1 truck = 14 feet, 9 inches (4.5 meters); 1 skunk = 8½ inches (22 centimeters)

An **NBA PLAYER** with a basketball

is almost as tall as

7 STYLISH DOLLS.

1 player = 6 ft., 8 in. (2 m); 1 doll = 1 ft. (30 cm)

470 CHATTERING CHIPMUNKS can be

as tall as

1 TOWERING REDWOOD TREE.

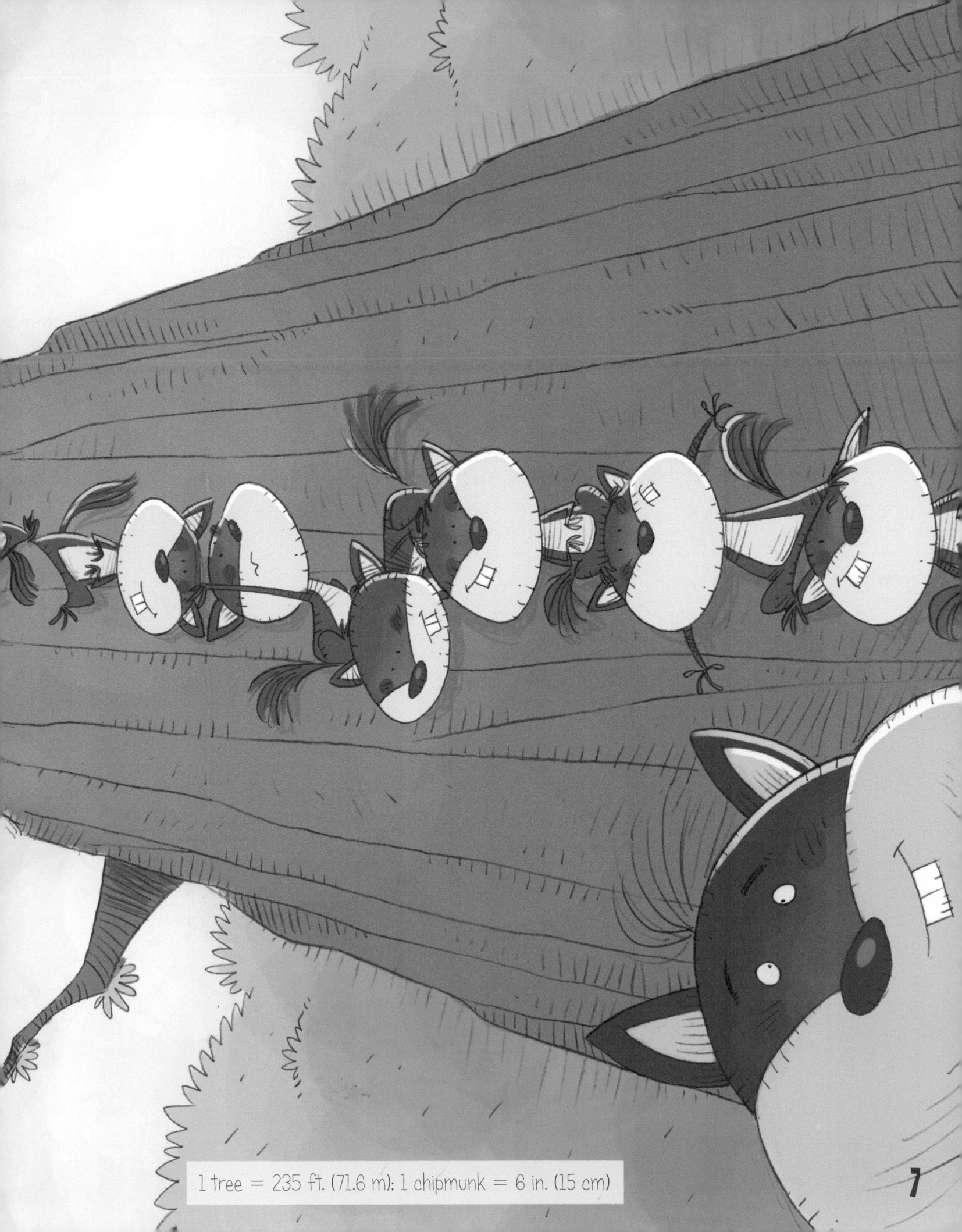

1 tree = 235 ft. (71.6 m); 1 chipmunk = 6 in. (15 cm)

To see to the top, we crane our necks.

36 HOT DOGS equal **1 T. REX!**

1 T. rex = 18 ft. (5.5 m); 1 hot dog = 6 in. (15 cm)

"The STATUE OF LIBERTY is tall. It's true!"

say 431 PIGEONS who wobble and coo.

1 statue = 305 ft. (93 m); 1 pigeon = 8½ in. (22 cm)

The **GREAT PYRAMID** has a height a bit greater than **84 REFRIGERATORS**.

1 pyramid = 450 ft. (137 m); 1 fridge = 5 ft., 4 in. (1.6 m)

Just clearing the height

of **1 GIRAFFE**,

14 TEDDY BEARS

stand tall and laugh.

1 giraffe = 17 ft. (5.2 m); 1 bear = 1 ft., 3 in. (38 cm)

1 OSTRICH, feathered and tall.

nearly equals the height of **11** SOCCER BALLS.

1 ostrich = 8 ft. (2.4 m); 1 ball = 9 in. (23 cm)

An **ELEPHANT**,

from bottom to top,

is as tall as **4 FIRE HYDRANTS**
that just won't stop!

1 elephant = 10 ft., 6 in. (3.2 m); 1 hydrant = 2 ft., 8 in. (81 cm)

The world's tallest mountain is

MOUNT EVEREST.

How many ELEPHANTS match

its snowy crest?

2,765

1 mountain = 29,035 ft. (8.8 kilometers); 1 elephant = 10 ft. 6 in. (3.2 m)

How many **POPSICLES** should you buy

to match the height of a **BIRD** that can't fly?